NO-SEW
FABRIC DÉCOR

NO-SEW
FABRIC DÉCOR

*Transform Your
Home without
Sewing a Stitch*

Pamela J. Hastings

**CREATIVE
PUBLISHING
international**

CHANHASSEN, MINNESOTA

ACKNOWLEDGMENTS

A special thank you to some special friends who helped me along the way to complete this book. To Kathy Sauter, Maggy Guinco, Becky Salaway, Pat Gaylor, and Karen Swider, thank you for letting me use your homes for photography and for helping me complete all the projects on time. To my family, thanks again for all your support and enthusiasm. Thanks also to Geoffrey Gross for the wonderful photography, to Jean McNiff for the beautiful illustrations, and to everyone at Creative Publishing international for your expertise and professionalism.

__ Pamela Hastings

President/CEO: Michael Eleftheriou
Vice President/Publisher: Linda Ball
Vice President/Retail Sales: Kevin Haas

Executive Editor: Alison Brown Cerier
Managing Editor: Yen Le
Art Director/Designer: Lois Stanfield
Senior Editor: Linda Neubauer
Copy Editor: Donna Hoel
Proofreader/Indexer: Catherine Broberg
Director of Production & Photography: Kim Gerber
Color Specialist: Tate Carlson
Photo Stylist: Patricia Gaylor

Photographer: Geoffrey Gross
Watercolor Illustrator: Jean M. McNiff

Library of Congress Cataloging-in-Publication Data

Hastings, Pamela J.
  No-sew fabric decor : transform your home without
  sewing a stitch / By Pamela J. Hastings.
       p. cm.
   Includes index.
   ISBN 1-58923-153-8 (sc)
   1. Household linens. 2. Fusible materials in sewing.
   3. Textile fabrics in interior decoration. I. Title.
   TT387.H3724 2004
   746.9--dc22

                        2004004621

Printed by R.R. Donnelley
10 9 8 7 6 5 4 3 2 1

CONTENTS

INTRODUCTION

ABOUT THE AUTHOR

Pamela J. Hastings has written six books on home décor sewing, including *Simple-to-Sew Slipcovers and Cover-Ups* and *Home Decorating Basics.* All have been selections of the Crafter's Choice Book Club. She is a spokesperson for Viking Sewing Machine, Velcro USA, Waverly, and Rowenta. Her sewing career began with ten years in the education department of Singer. Pamela appears regularly on home shows and has written articles for such magazines as *Family Circle, Woman's Day, Good Housekeeping,* and *Better Homes and Gardens.* She lives in New Jersey.

Do you have a home to decorate, but don't sew?
You're certainly not alone. Lots of people just never learned how. Others find that their sewing skills are "rusty" or they don't have a sewing machine. You're also not alone in your desire to make home décor items like window treatments, linens, and home accessories. Many people are not satisfied with the choices in ready-made items, but are shocked by the cost of ordering custom versions.

No-Sew Fabric Décor features techniques and projects that will help you make real curtains and valances, cover-ups, bed and bath linens, pillows, and home accessories *without sewing a single stitch.* The step-by-step, illustrated projects make it easy to transform a room armed only with no-sew products such as glue, staples, grommets, fusible webs, and hook and loop tape.

I have to admit I was skeptical at first when approached to write this book. After all, I love to sew, have written books on sewing for the home, and even work for sewing-industry companies. I wondered whether décor sewing projects could be adapted in a way that made sense, and with results that I would be proud to have in my own home. As I looked into the possibilities, though, I grew excited. I discovered that many fabric décor items can be created without sewing. No-sew techniques are sometimes easier or faster, and some projects can *only* be made this way.

I've developed a wide range of projects. Some are quick and very easy; they're just the thing if you're decorating your first apartment, a dorm room, or a vacation home. Some of the projects are a bit more involved, but will allow you to turn high-end fabrics and trims into fabulous décor.

In the first chapter, you will learn about the tools and supplies you need. You'll also learn basic techniques and some important tips, so read through this section before beginning.

Then you'll be ready to pick your first project. If you want to dress a window, look through the first group of projects. Café curtains from tea towels and spruced-up ready-made curtains are great starter projects. Elegant options include swags and upholstered cornice boards. The next group of projects offers slipcovers and table linens, plus directions for reupholstering a worn dining chair with updated fabric and a staple gun. In the bed and bath section are such projects as an upholstered headboard, bed skirt, and shower curtain. The last group is a variety of accessories, from lampshades and pillows to an armoire embellished with panels of fabric.

Throughout the book you will find variations of the projects with even more decorating ideas. Mix and match techniques and ideas to create your own one-of-a-kind, "where did you get that?" home decorating items.

Creating something beautiful for yourself is what sewing is all about. Now you can enjoy personalizing your living space and enhancing its comfort—and you won't have to sew at all.

Pamela J. Hastings

GETTING STARTED

No-sew fabric décor is easy, once you know about a few simple tools and techniques. Before you start any project, read this chapter to familiarize yourself with the special tools and materials and learn some basic methods. You'll be happier with your results if you do.

When you use a no-sew technique for the first time, it's a good idea to practice on a scrap of fabric. For example, if you are installing grommets, experiment on a scrap so you won't make a mistake on your finished piece.

Another thing that makes a big difference in your final results is to spend a little extra time choosing fabrics and other materials. There are so many wonderful fabrics out there and so many trims to give your project the right look.

You can have professional-looking results if you use the right materials and tools—and use them correctly. Fortunately, no-sew decorating doesn't require a lot of unusual equipment. You probably have a lot of these tools already. You won't need to buy a sewing machine!

BASIC TOOLS

Iron (a) Perhaps the most important tool in no-sew decorating is your iron. Pressing is the key to avoiding the "homemade" look. In no-sew decorating, your iron not only makes your fabric crisp, but also fuses seams and secures trims. Be sure your iron works well at various temperature settings and can be used as both a dry and a steam iron. Some fusible tapes require steam, others a dry iron. A "burst of steam" feature is great for creating firm folds and creases on the edges of your fabric.

Shears (b) Dressmaker shears, with blades 8" or 9" (20.5 or 23 cm) long, are designed to cut through several layers of fabric at a time or a single layer of heavy fabric. Shears should be sharp, so they can cut through fabric easily without tearing it.

Staple Gun (c) A staple gun is essential for projects such as ottomans and headboards. Stapling fabric allows you to pull it firmly and secure it to a wood surface.

Scissors (d) Scissors are used for small cutting tasks such as trimming fabric edges or cutting trims to length. Be sure your scissors are sharp and can cut easily from the base of the blade to the tip.

Hot Glue Gun (e) A hot glue gun heats a stick of glue to its melting point, then releases the glue when the trigger is pulled. Use a hot glue gun where fusible tapes are not appropriate, such as applying buttons or cording.

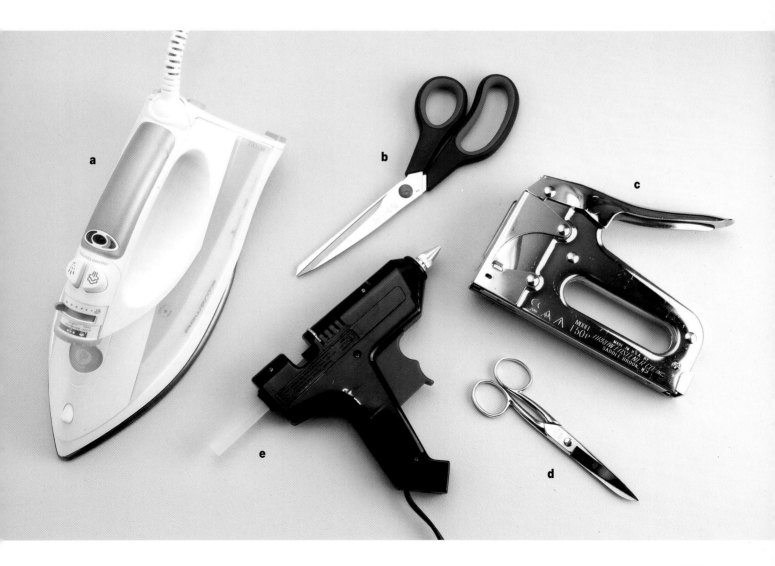

Grommet Setting Tool As the name implies, a grommet setting tool is used for attaching grommets to fabric. Grommet setting tools are available as a handheld "punch" or in separate pieces that must be struck with a mallet.

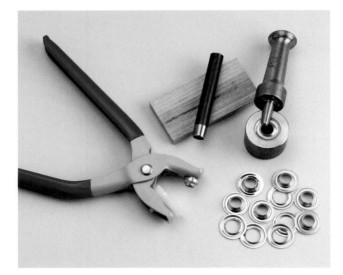

Bias Tape Maker This tool helps you make custom bias trim. Bias strips are cut to twice the desired finished width and then inserted through the tool. The bias tape maker folds in the edges while you press them in place with an iron. Bias tape makers are available in several widths, from 1/4" to 3" (6 mm to 7.5 cm).

MEASURING AND MARKING TOOLS

Tape Measure (a) Because they are flexible, cloth tape measures are used to measure curved areas, such as the edge of a seat or a round table. They are also suitable for measuring soft items like pillows.

Fabric Marker (b) Use a water-soluble marker to mark the placement of hems and trims. Marks can be removed with a few drops of water when they are no longer needed.

Metal Tape Measure (c) Metal tape measures hold their shape and are often longer than cloth measuring tapes or yardsticks. Use metal tape measures for areas that need to be measured accurately, such as tabletops and windows.

Yardstick (d) A yardstick (meterstick), which is 36 inches (100 centimeters) long, can be used for measuring fabric and smaller items.

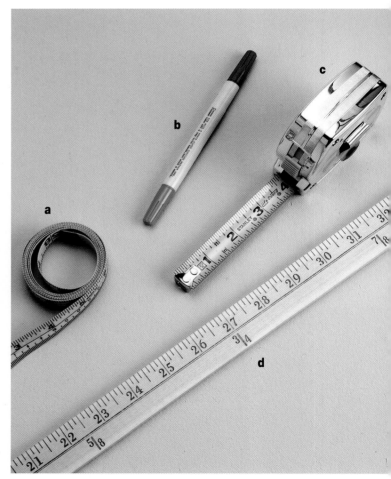

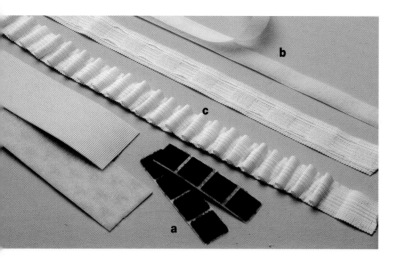

FASTENING TAPES

Heavy-duty Hook and Loop Tape (a) This tape, which has an adhesive backing, is ideal for connecting two hard surfaces when nails or staples are not appropriate.

Traditional Hook and Loop Tape (b) Although made to be sewn on, this fastener can also be attached with fusible tape. Use hook and loop tape for attaching bed skirts or for closures on slipcovers or pillows. There is also tape with a plain hook tape and an adhesive-backed loop tape; use this when attaching a fabric to a hard surface.

Styling Tape (c) This is used to gather or pleat fabric. The tape is fused to the back side of the fabric, then cords in the tape are pulled to create the desired effect.

FUSIBLE WEB, TAPES, AND GLUES

Test fabrics and fusible webs or glues to be sure the product you have chosen does not discolor or pucker your fabric.

Fusible Web (a) Fusible web is used for seaming, hemming, and applying trims. Fusible web is sold by the roll or sheet in a variety of widths and strengths. The type backed with paper is easiest to work with. The product is placed on the fabric, fusible side down, and ironed on the paper backing. The heat of the iron melts the fusible web and makes it stick to your fabric, but not the paper, which is then easily peeled away. The exposed web is then fused to another fabric or trim. To determine which product to use for your project, think about the product's end use. If you are embellishing a towel that will be laundered frequently, use a fusible web with the strongest bond. If you are hemming a sheer fabric, use a softer fusible that won't leave a stiff edge. Directions for using fusible webs and tapes (for example, which heat setting to use) may vary from manufacturer to manufacturer, so be sure to read all the directions carefully.

Adhesive Tape (b) Adhesive tape is used for seaming, hemming, and applying trim. Press the tape onto the fabric with your fingers, then remove the paper backing to expose the adhesive. Apply the next layer and again finger-press in place. You can also iron and heat-set for a stronger bond. Like fusible web, adhesive tape is available in a variety of widths and strengths.

Spray Foam Adhesive (c) Spray adhesive is used to secure foam and batting in upholstered projects.

Fabric Glue (d) This product can be used to adhere fabric and trims. Fabric glue may loosen after several washings, so it may not be suitable for all projects.

Liquid Fray Preventer (not shown) This colorless plastic liquid prevents fraying by stiffening the fabric slightly. It may darken some colors, so test before using and apply carefully. The liquid may be removed with rubbing alcohol. It dries to a permanent finish that can be washed or dry-cleaned.

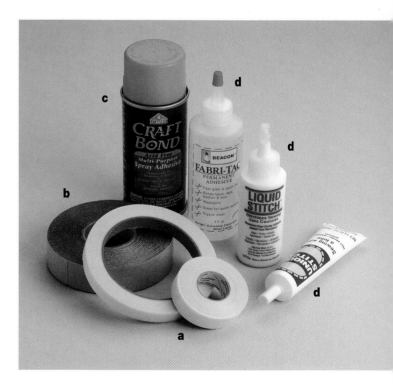

ATTACHING GROMMETS

1. Fold under the edge of the fabric the required amount and press. Mark the placement of the grommets and cut the opening, using the grommet cutting tool.

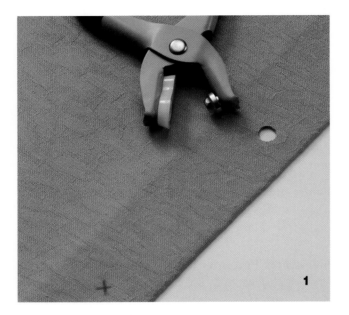

2. Insert the male side of the grommet through the hole from the right side to the wrong side of the fabric. Place the grommet ring over the post and secure with the grommet setting tool.

MAKING A DOUBLE-FOLD HEM

1. Measure and fold up the hem amount and press in place. Add twice the hem amount to your project measurements. For example, if you are making a 1" (2.5 cm) double-fold hem, add 2" (5 cm) to your project measurement.

2. Fuse a strip of paper-backed fusible web along the pressed edge of the hem, following the manufacturer's directions. Remove the paper backing.

3. Fold the hem again, the same amount, and fuse in place.

GLUING TRIM

Hot-gluing with a glue gun works well for attaching cording and trim, especially in areas where pressing isn't possible, such as the edge of an ottoman. You can also apply trim with fabric glue using the same method.

1. Measure and draw a placement line for the trim, using a fabric marker.

2. Working a few inches (centimeters) at a time, run a bead of hot glue along the marked line. Immediately finger-press your trim along the hot glue. Hold in place a few seconds to be sure it is secure.

ATTACHING TRIM WITH FUSIBLE WEB

This method of applying trim works well for flat trims or ribbons and on long lengths of fabric that can be easily pressed.

1. Measure and draw a placement line for the trim, using a fabric marker.

2. Center the paper-backed fusible web over the marked line; fuse, following the manufacturer's directions.

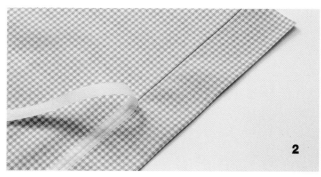

3. Remove the paper backing. Place the trim over the fusible web and fuse in place with an iron.

FABRICS AND TRIMS

Most home decorating projects—sew or no-sew—are best made with special fabrics designed for this purpose. Home decorating fabrics are usually 54" to 60" (137 to 152.5 cm) wide and are treated to resist soiling and creasing. They are often available in collections, making it easy to select coordinating designs.

Home decorating fabrics come in various weights for various uses. Upholstery-weight fabrics are heavy and durable. Drapery fabrics are mediumweight and can be used for almost any project, from window treatments to tablecloths to bed skirts.

If you are making something that requires fabric wider than 60" (152.5 cm), such as a bed skirt or headboard, you may be able to cut the material with the lengthwise grain (parallel to the finished edges) running horizontally rather than vertically. This is called railroading. Fabric with an all-over design that has no distinct direction can be railroaded. Solids, plaids, and checks are also good choices.

Some garment fabrics can also be used in home decorating. Eyelet, cotton prints, and piqués are perfect for window valances and pillows.

Sheets, napkins, placemats, or tea towels also can be used for no-sew projects. Beautiful linens available in a wide variety of colors and styles are perfect for many of these projects.

An interesting trim can add just the right touch to a decorating project. There are lots of trims to suit every style. The projects in this book use a variety of trims and embellishments. You can also experiment with the many possibilities. Use lush bullion fringe for a dramatic look or simple grosgrain ribbon for a casual country look. Charms, buttons, and beads can add an unexpected detail to window treatments and chair covers. Toggle closures and frogs are a decorative as well as functional detail on the edges of fitted projects. Try adding a tassel to the end of a tablecloth or pointed valance. Paint and rubber stamps can provide a whimsical or sophisticated finishing touch.

WINDOW TREATMENTS

> Grommeted Roman Shade

> Ribboned Valance

> Custom Roller Shade

> Color Block Panel

> Tent-Flap Curtain

> Tea Towel Café Curtains

> Padded Cornice

> Teardrop Swag

> Scarf Swag with Beaded Trim

> Curtains with Netting
Border

> Faux Suede Valance

> *Fusing*
> *Grommets*

GROMMETED ROMAN SHADE

MATERIALS

Mediumweight
decorator fabric

Lining fabric

Paper-backed fusible web,
1/2" (1.3 cm) wide

Cord, 1/4" (6 mm) diameter,
two times the finished length
of the shade plus 20" (51 cm)

Grommets,
3/8" (1 cm) diameter

Curtain rod, 1"
(2.5 cm) diameter

TOOLS

Metal tape measure

Yardstick (meterstick)

Shears

Iron

Fabric marker

Grommet setting tool

In this tailored shade, the cording threaded through a series of grommets is both decorative and functional. To raise the shade, simply push the fabric up along the cords and knot the cords. To lower the shade, untie the knots.

Cording is available in many colors. For patterned or striped shades, select a solid cord in an accent color. For a shade made in a solid fabric, consider a cord in a twist of several colors.

The shade may be mounted inside the window frame on a spring tension rod or outside the frame on a decorative rod. Mount the curtain rod before measuring the dimensions of your shade.

> *How to Make a Grommeted Roman Shade*

CUTTING

- Measure the length and width of the window. Cut decorator fabric and lining as wide as the finished shade plus 4" (10 cm) and as long as the finished shade plus 6" (15 cm).

- Cut two lengths of cord the length of the finished shade plus 10" (25.5 cm).

1. Place the lining and fabric, wrong sides together, on a flat surface. Turn under and press a 1" (2.5 cm) double-fold hem on each side. Secure with paper-backed fusible web (page 12).

2. Make a 1½" (3.8 cm) double-fold hem on the bottom of the shade.

3. Turn under and press ½" (1.3 cm) and then another 1½" (3.8 cm) on the shade top, forming a rod pocket. Secure along the narrow fold, using fusible web.

4. Mark an uneven number of Xs in two columns on the lining side of the shade, 8" to 9" (20.5 to 23 cm) from the sides, for the grommet placements. Start just above the bottom hem and space the others evenly 6" to 8" (15 to 20.5 cm) apart.

5. Install the grommets at the marks (page 12).

6. Knot one end of each cord. Beginning at the bottom front of the shade, thread each cord through the grommets. Knot the other end of each cord at the top back of the shade, and trim close to the knots.

7. Insert the curtain rod through the rod pocket and hang the shade. Slide the shade along the cords to the desired height and tie knots to hold it in place.

For a soft, feminine shade that will be stationary, use ribbon instead of grommets and cording. Construct the shade in the same way but skip the steps for the grommets. Cut two lengths of ribbon twice the length of the finished shade. Fold each length of ribbon in half, crosswise, and fuse to the top of the shade. Fanfold the shade to the desired height, and tie the ribbons into a knot or bow.

> *Fusing*
> *Grommets*

RIBBONED VALANCE

MATERIALS

Decorative curtain rod

Mediumweight
decorator fabric

Paper-backed fusible web,
1/2" (1.3 cm) wide

Grommets,
3/4" (2 cm) diameter

Ribbon, about 2 1/2 times the
window width

Shells

TOOLS

Metal tape measure

Yardstick (meterstick)

Shears

Iron

Fabric marker

Grommet setting tool

Hot glue gun

Grommets make this versatile valance easy.
Ribbon is strung through the grommets and
over a decorative rod to hold the valance in
place. The valance can be flat or have only
slight fullness, making it a perfect choice for a
colorful printed fabric. For a little girl's room,
choose a whimsical print and decorate with
shells or beads, as shown. For a masculine
look, hang a denim valance with striped or
plaid ribbon. Use a lightweight sheer fabric
and sheer ribbons for a romantic look. If your
window is very wide, look for a fabric that can
be railroaded (page 14) to avoid having a seam.
The possibilities are endless.

> How to Make a Ribboned Valance

CUTTING

- Install the curtain rod high enough above the window so the valance covers the top of the window frame.

- Cut the fabric 1½ times the width of the rod plus 2" (5 cm) and twice the desired valance length plus 3" (7.5 cm).

1. Turn under and press 1" (2.5 cm) to the wrong side of the fabric along each side edge of the valance.

2. Fold the valance in half crosswise, wrong sides together, aligning the top and bottom edges. Fuse in place along the sides with strips of ½" (1.3 cm) fusible web.

3. Make a 1½" (3.8 cm) double-fold hem at the top of the valance (page 12).

4. Mark the placement of the grommets along the top of the valance. Grommets should be placed about 5" (12.7 cm) apart with the outer grommets 1½" (3.8 cm) from the sides. Install grommets at markings (page 12).

5. Lay curtain rod and valance on a flat surface. Beginning at one end of the valance, insert the ribbon from the back of the grommet to the front. Loop the ribbon over the rod and back through the front of the first grommet; tie a knot on the back and secure with hot glue. Continue by wrapping the ribbon over the rod and into each grommet. Keep the distance between the bottom of the rod and the top of the valance even.

6. Tie the ribbon in a knot behind the last grommet and secure with hot glue. Glue shells just below the first and last grommets.

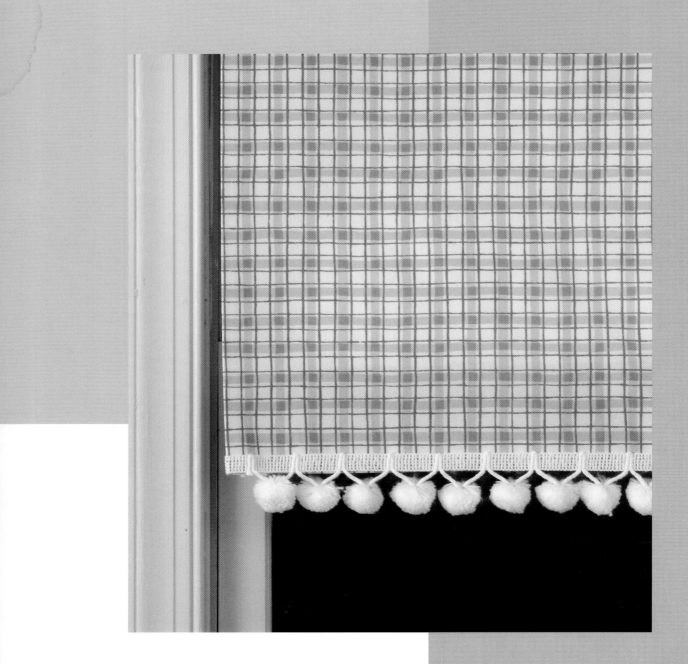

> *Fusing*

CUSTOM ROLLER SHADE

MATERIALS

Shade roller and hardware

Mediumweight decorator fabric

Fusible shade backing

Liquid fray preventer

Paper-backed fusible web, 1/2" (1.3 cm) wide

Ball fringe

Adhesive tape if roller is metal

Flat wood strip, 3/4" (2 cm) wide by width of shade

TOOLS

Yardstick (meterstick)

Shears

Iron

Staple gun and 1/2" (1.3 cm) staples

It's easy to make a custom roller shade. You simply attach fabric to a fusible shade backing sold in fabric stores. Use the roller and brackets from an old shade or buy an inexpensive shade just for the roller. Roller shade kits that include the fusible backing, brackets, and shade roller are also available.

Mediumweight fabrics work best for this project. Avoid fabrics with an added glaze or water-repellant finish, as they may not fuse evenly. To block out light, select a tightly woven dark fabric. Add decorative braid, fringe, or ribbon to the bottom of your shade for a finishing touch.

CUTTING

- Mount the shade brackets and roller. Cut the fabric 4" (10 cm) wider than the roller and 12" (30.5 cm) longer than the window length.

- Cut shade backing as wide as the roller and 12" (30.5 cm) longer than the window length.

1. Place fabric, right side down, on a flat surface. Center the shade backing, fusible side down, on the wrong side of the fabric. Fuse in place, following the manufacturer's instructions.

2. Trim the sides of the fabric even with the shade backing. Seal the cut edges with liquid fray preventer, if necessary.

3. Turn under 1/2" (1.3 cm), then 1" (2.5 cm) at the bottom to form a casing. Fuse in place.

4. Cut a length of ball fringe or other trim equal to the width of the shade plus 1" (2.5 cm). Turn under 1/2" (1.3 cm) at the cut ends of the trim and glue or fuse it to the right side of the lower edge of the shade (page 13).

5. Lay shade, backing side down, on a flat surface. Place shade roller a few inches from the top of the shade. Wrap the top of the shade around the roller and secure with staples (if using a wooden roller) or tape (if using a metal roller).

6. Insert the wood strip into the casing and hang the shade.

> *Fusing*

COLOR BLOCK PANEL

MATERIALS

Decorative curtain rod

Ready-made drapery panel in the dimensions required for your window

Mediumweight decorator fabric for contrasting bands

Paper-backed fusible web, 1/2" (1.3 cm) wide

TOOLS

Yardstick (meterstick)

Fabric marker

Shears

Iron

Another no-sew strategy is to start with a basic purchased item. You can buy a plain drapery panel and dress it up with a band or border in a contrasting color. Choose a fabric with a weight and feel similar to that of the drapery. If you plan to machine wash the drapery later, prewash both the drapery and the contrasting fabrics before making the new panels.

To determine the placement of the contrasting fabric, hang the panel and hold up the contrasting fabric to see what looks good to you. As a general rule, the bottom band should be about one-third of the total length of a floor-length panel.

> *How to Make a Color Block Panel*

1. Lay the drapery panel on a flat surface. Draw a horizontal line 12" to 15" (30.5 to 38 cm) from the top edge. Measure up from the hem the desired amount and subtract ½" (1.3 cm); draw a second horizontal line at this point.

2. Cut along the lower horizontal line.

3. Cut a piece of contrasting fabric as wide as the drapery panel plus 2" (5 cm) and as long as the cut-away portion plus 2½" (6.5 cm). Cut a 4" (10 cm) band of contrasting fabric as wide as the panel plus 2" (5 cm).

4. Turn ½" (1.3 cm) to the right side of the drapery panel along the cut edge. Fuse in place.

5. Turn up a 1" (2.5 cm) double-fold hem along the bottom of the longer contrasting fabric (page 12). Turn under and press ½" (1.3 cm) along the upper edge of the fabric and fuse in place.

6. Overlap the ½" (1.3 cm) folds on the drapery panel and the contrasting band and fuse in place. The contrasting fabric will extend 1" (2.5 cm) beyond each side of the drapery panel.

7. Turn under a ½" (1.3 cm) double-fold hem along each side of the contrasting fabric.

8. Turn under and press ½" (1.3 cm) along each long edge of the contrasting band.

9. Make a ½" (1.3 cm) double-fold hem on each side of the band and fuse in place. Center the band over the top marked line and fuse in place.

> *Fusing*

TENT-FLAP CURTAIN

MATERIALS

Spring tension rod or decorative curtain rod

Mediumweight decorator fabric for the front

Mediumweight contrasting decorator fabric for the back and front border

Paper-backed fusible web, 1/2" (1.3 cm) wide

Remnant of cord

Decorative drapery hook

TOOLS

Metal tape measure

Yardstick (meterstick)

Shears

Iron

This curtain panel is held open with a drapery hook and can be released and closed for privacy. The front and back are coordinating fabrics, and when the curtain is open, both are seen. Choose toile and checks for a French country style, dots and stripes for a child's room, even two solid jewel tones for a dramatic look. Be sure the back fabric does not show through the front and the fabrics have similar weights.

CUTTING

- Hang the curtain rod. Measure the length and width of the area to be covered. Cut the curtain back to these measurements plus 4" (10 cm) in both directions.

- Cut the front fabric to the finished width plus 4" (10 cm) and the finished length plus 3" (7.5 cm).

1. Turn under and press a 1" (2.5 cm) double-fold hem (page 12) on the sides of the back panel but do not fuse. Lay the fabric wrong side up on a flat surface. Open out the folded edges and place the front panel right side up on the back fabric, aligning the edges of the front to the inside folds. Refold the side hems and fuse in place.

2. At the top of the panel, turn under ½" (1.3 cm) and then 1" (2.5 cm) to form a rod pocket. Fuse in place.

3. At the bottom of the panel, turn under 1/2" (1.3 cm) and press. Then turn the corners in diagonally 1" (2.5 cm) from the bottom to miter.

4. Turn up a 1" (2.5 cm) hem along the bottom; tuck a loop of cord into one mitered corner. Fuse the hem in place, catching the cord ends in the fusible web.

5. Hang the curtain. Pull back the loop corner to determine the placement for the decorative hanger. Insert the hanger in the wall.

> *Gluing*

TEA TOWEL CAFÉ CURTAINS

MATERIALS

Café rod or spring tension rod

Tea towels

Rickrack

Fabric glue

Decorative clip-on curtain rings

TOOLS

Metal tape measure

Fabric marker

Iron

It's quick and easy to turn tea towels into café curtains for your kitchen. With this method, you don't even need to cut the towels. The window size determines how many towels you need and whether the towels should be placed horizontally or vertically. Hold the towel up to the window to see if you prefer a full or flat look. Fold the top forward until the bottom rests on the window sill, add some decorative trim, and enjoy. Tea towels are available in many fun colors and patterns; create several sets of curtains and change them with the seasons. Hang the curtains from a café rod using simple metal clip-on rings or some cheerful decorative curtain clips.

> *How to Make Tea Towel Café Curtains*

1. Install the café rod at the desired height. Using a metal tape measure, measure from the bottom of the rod to the windowsill.

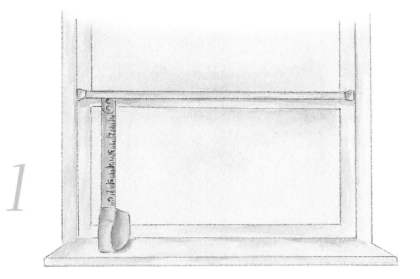

1

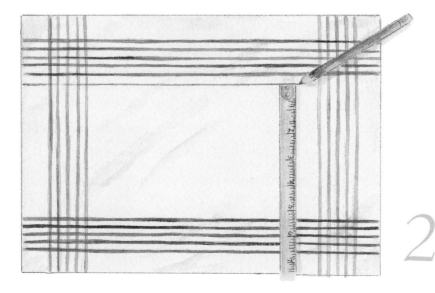

2

2. Lay the tea towel on a flat surface. Measure up from the bottom and draw a line equal to the measurement in step 1.

3. Fold the towel forward along the line and press in place forming a valance. Glue rickrack along the lower edge of the valance.

4. Place clip-on rings over the café rod and clip them to the upper folded edge of the curtain.

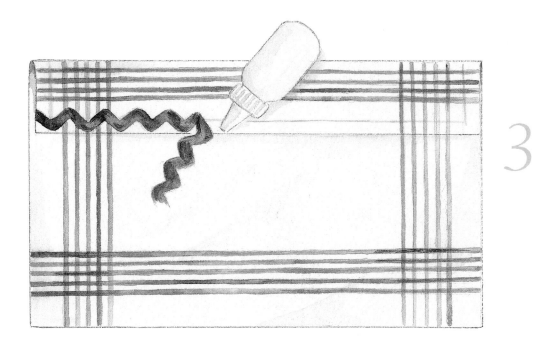

> *Basic Carpentry*
> *Stapling*
> *Gluing*

PADDED CORNICE

MATERIALS

Plywood, 1/4" (6 mm) thick, cut to size

2 × 4 board cut to size

Wood glue

Finishing nails, 1 1/2" (3.8 cm) long

Upholstery batting, 1" (2.5 cm) thick

Spray adhesive

Mediumweight decorator fabric, enough to cover the cornice box

Lining for the inside of the cornice box

Decorative cording

3" × 3" (7.5 × 7.5 cm) angle brackets and screws

TOOLS

Metal tape measure

Saw

Hammer

Staple gun and staples

Shears

Iron

Hot glue gun

A padded cornice is a simple yet stylish window topper. Fabric and batting are stapled over a wooden cornice box. A cornice is perfect with wood blinds or decorative shades because it hides the hardware. Your home improvement store will cut the lumber to size for you.

For a child's room, you can make a cornice that coordinates with bedding by using a matching flat sheet. Faux suede makes a great cornice for a den or home office. If the fabric is solid or has an all-over print, you can railroad it if necessary (page 14). If you need to seam the fabric, put a seam at each side of the cornice rather than one in the center, following step 1 on page 100.

> How to Make a Padded Cornice

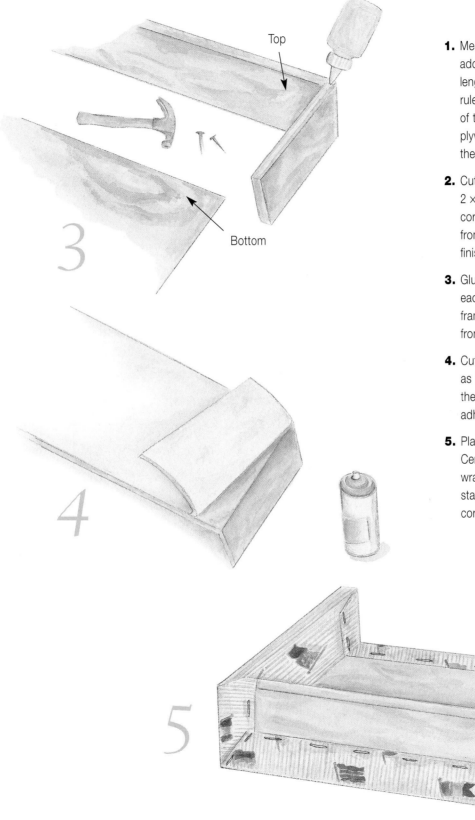

Top

Bottom

3

4

5

1. Measure the width of the window and add 4" (10 cm). Determine the desired length of the cornice. As a general rule, a cornice should be one-fifth of the window treatment length. Cut plywood for the front of the cornice to the desired finished height and width.

2. Cut two cornice end pieces from the 2 × 4 that are the height of the finished cornice. Cut the top of the cornice from the 2 × 4 to the width of the finished cornice minus 1½" (3.8 cm).

3. Glue and then nail an end piece to each end of the top piece to create a frame. Glue and then nail the cornice front over the frame.

4. Cut a piece of batting the same size as the cornice front and sides. Cover the cornice with batting, using spray adhesive.

5. Place fabric facedown on a flat surface. Center the cornice box over the fabric, wrap the fabric around the box, and staple it in place on the inside of the cornice box.

6. Cut the lining to the dimensions of the inside of the cornice box, plus 1" (2.5 cm). Turn under 1/2" (1.3 cm) along the edge of the lining and staple in place.

7. Cut a piece of fabric or lining equal to the measurement of the top of the cornice plus 1" (2.5 cm). Turn under and press with iron 1/2" (1.3 cm) on all edges. Place fabric over the top of the cornice and staple in place.

8. Tie a knot in the cording and hot-glue in place at the back edge of the cornice. Repeat at the front corner. Tie knots across the front of the cornice, spacing them equal distances apart. Add another knot at corner and back edge on other side.

9. Secure angle irons to the top under-side of the cornice. Mark placement of screw holes on the wall. Remove angle irons, and install on the wall. Place cornice on angle irons and screw in place.

> *Fusing*

> *Gluing*

TEARDROP SWAG

MATERIALS

Kraft paper

Light- or mediumweight decorator fabric

Paper-backed fusible web, 1/2" (1.3 cm) wide

Button tassel

Drapery pins

TOOLS

Metal tape measure

Marker

Ruler or yardstick (meterstick)

Pins

Shears

Iron

Hot glue gun

A teardrop swag defines simple elegance. This treatment can be used alone or can top shutters, a shade, or blinds. For wide windows, you can make more than one swag and overlap the ends before pinning in place.

The swag is simply a diamond shape folded in half. For solid colors and nondirectional prints, cut the fabric so the fold is on the bias (45-degree angle to the selvages). This allows the swag to drape gracefully. Directional prints should be cut so the pattern is straight.

The swag is attached to the window frame with decorative drapery pins. You can buy these or make your own by gluing a decorative button to the head of a small nail.

> *How to Make a Teardrop Swag*

1. Determine where on the window frame you will hang the swag. Measure the width of the area to be covered and add 4" to 5" (10 to 12.7 cm). Measure from the top of the window frame down to the desired length.

2. Make a pattern for the swag using the above measurements. Draw a line on kraft paper equal to the width above. From the midpoint of the line, measure down and mark a point equal to the length. Using a ruler or yardstick, join the point to the ends of the line, forming a triangle. Add a 1/2" (1.3 cm) seam allowance along the side lines.

3. Fold the fabric in half (crosswise or diagonally as determined by the design). Pin the pattern on the fabric, with the top edge of the swag even with the fold. Cut along the outer line.

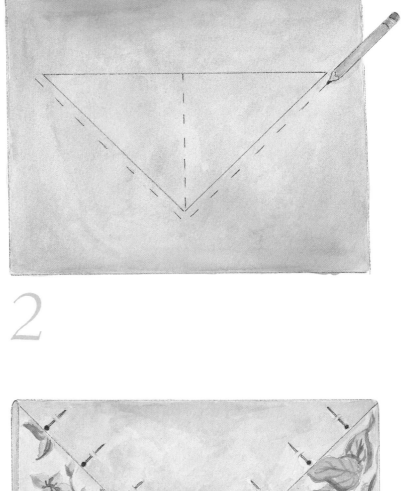

2

3

4. Turn under and press ½" (1.3 cm) to the wrong side of the fabric along the edges of the swag. (Note: Top and bottom angles will be evenly pressed; side angles will have fabric extending beyond the edge.)

5. Open the side edges, fold the point in ½" (1.3 cm), and press.

6. Refold the fabric along the original lines and press.

7. Fold the swag in half, wrong sides together, matching the folded edges. Fuse the edges together with paper-backed fusible web.

8. Center the tassel at the lower corner of the swag and attach, using a hot glue gun. Hang the swag on the window frame with drapery pins.

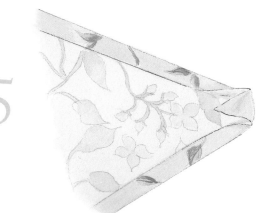

> *Fusing*

SCARF SWAG WITH BEADED TRIM

MATERIALS

Swag holders

String

Mediumweight decorator fabric

Beaded trim (enough to go around the bottom and sides of the swag)

Paper-backed fusible web, 1/2" (1.3 cm) wide

TOOLS

Yardstick (meterstick)

Fabric marker

Shears

Iron

Scarf swags are a simple version of the traditional swag and jabot. They can be formal or casual depending on the fabric. Medium-weight fabrics drape better than heavy ones. Trim the bottom with beads for a trendy look.

The treatment is a continuous rectangle of fabric draped over swag holders. Mount the holders at the corners of the window frame or outside the frame a few inches above the window. Install the hardware before measuring the scarf length to determine how long the sides should be. The rule of thumb is that the sides should either reach the window sill or extend two-thirds the length of the window.

> *How to Make a Scarf Swag with Beaded Trim*

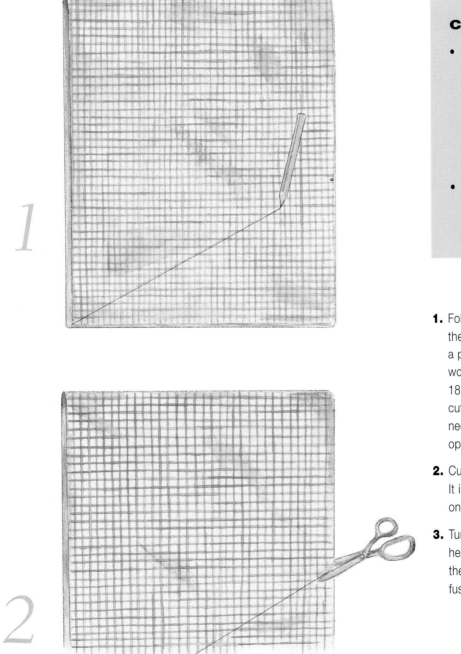

CUTTING

- Hang swag holders in the desired locations. Drape a string between the holders and down the sides of the window to the desired swag length. Remove the string and measure.

- Cut a length of fabric to the length of the string plus 1" (2.5 cm).

1. Fold fabric in half crosswise, aligning the raw edges. Measure and mark a point along the selvage (tightly woven edge of the fabric) about 18" to 20" (46 to 51 cm) from the cut ends. Draw a diagonal line connecting the marked point and the opposite corner of the fabric.

2. Cut the fabric along the marked line. It is a good idea to cut the fabric one layer at a time.

3. Turn under a single-fold 1/2" (1.3 cm) hem on all edges of the scarf. Fuse the hem in place with paper-backed fusible web.

A DIFFERENT LOOK

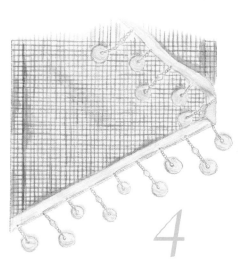

4. Attach trim to the wrong side of the swag over the hem, using paper-backed fusible web (page 13).

5. On a flat surface, fanfold the swag. Place the swag over the holders and arrange the center and sides.

For a more casual look, make a scarf swag from an all-over print. Instead of swag holders, use wrought iron holdbacks, traditionally used to hold open floor-length curtains. Angle the holdbacks so that the swag will stay in place. If you're making a swag without trim, fuse a double-fold hem on the lower edge to hide the raw edge of the fabric.

> *Gluing*

CURTAINS WITH NETTING BORDER

MATERIALS

Ready-made valance and café curtains

Liquid fray preventer

Netting or tulle

Fabric glue

Foam shapes

Rickrack (enough to cover the width of the valance and curtains)

TOOLS

Ruler or yardstick (meterstick)

Shears

Fabric marker

Look through the netting at the bottom of these curtains and you see bright colors and fun shapes! This is an interesting way to spruce up plain curtains. Craft stores sell these foam shapes in many sizes and themes. They also sell sheets of foam in case you want to design your own shapes. An aquatic theme like this one is perfect for a bathroom. Cars and trucks would make the curtains suitable for a little boy's room. A teenager might prefer bright daisy shapes in the netting and ball fringe in place of the rickrack.

Permanent fabric glue, rather than fusible adhesive, is used to attach the netting and foam shapes because netting will melt under a hot iron.

CUTTING

- Measure up from the bottom of the valance and cut off 5" (12.7 cm). Repeat with the curtains. Seal the cut edges of fabric with liquid fray preventer.

- Cut an 11" (28 cm) strip of netting to match the width of the valance plus 1" (2.5 cm). Cut a strip for each curtain panel the width of the curtain plus 1" (2.5 cm).

1. Mark a line ½" (1.3 cm) from each long edge of each netting strip. Fold the strips in half lengthwise and finger-press.

2. Open the netting and lay it on a flat surface. Using fabric glue, secure foam shapes in the desired locations between the foldline and the upper marked line. After gluing, turn the netting over so the glue is facing up and will not stick to your work surface. Allow glue to dry completely, according to manufacturer's directions.

3. Refold the netting over the foam shapes. Sandwich the netting strip over the cut edge of the valance, overlapping the edges by 1/2" (1.3 cm). The ends of the strip should extend 1/2" (1.3 cm) beyond the edge of the valance. Secure with fabric glue. Repeat with the curtain panels.

4. Fold the edges of netting to the wrong side and lightly glue.

5. Cut a length of rickrack the width of the valance plus 1" (2.5 cm). Glue in place over the top edge of the netting, folding 1/2" (1.3 cm) to the wrong side at each end of the valance. Repeat for the curtain panels.

SUPER-QUICK NO-SEW

Faux Suede Valance

1. Install curtain rod at desired location. Cut squares of kraft paper and drape them over the rod. Adjust sizes as needed to determine the size of the finished squares.

2. Lay the pattern squares on faux suede and trace around the outside edge. Cut along the marked line.

3. Lay faux suede square on a flat surface and glue a decorative button, charm, or tassel at lower corner, using a hot glue gun.

4. Drape faux suede squares over curtain rod.

MATERIALS

Decorative curtain rod

Kraft paper

Faux suede in two colors

Decorative buttons,
charms, or tassels
(one for each fabric square)

TOOLS

Ruler or yardstick
(meterstick)

Fabric marker

Scissors

Hot glue gun

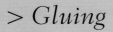

> *Gluing*

COVER-UPS

> *Fusing*

ROUND TABLE SKIRT

MATERIALS

King-size flat sheet

Paper-backed fusible web, 1/2" (1.3 cm) wide

Fabric glue (optional)

Decorative trim, about 3¼ times the table skirt diameter (optional)

TOOLS

Shears

Yardstick (meterstick)

Fabric marker

String

T-pin

Iron

Flat sheets provide the perfect fabric for round tablecloths. You can select a coordinating sheet and make napkins or a square table topper.

The measurement from the edge of a table to the bottom of a tablecloth is called the drop length. There are three popular drop lengths for tablecloths. Short tablecloths are 10" (25.5 cm) long and fall to the top of chair seats. These are perfect for everyday. Mid-length cloths are more formal and have a drop of about 24" (61 cm). Floor-length cloths, used for decorator tables, are 28" to 29" (71 to 73.5 cm) long, depending on the height of the table. The finished size of the tablecloth is the diameter of the table plus twice the desired drop length.

> *How to Make a Round Table Skirt*

2

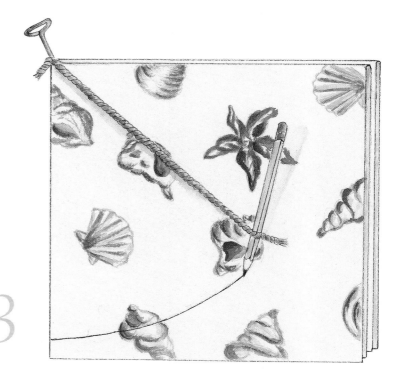

3

1. Cut a square of fabric equal to the diameter of the finished tablecloth (the diameter of the table plus twice the drop length) plus 1" (2.5 cm) for hems. For example, if your finished tablecloth will be 90" (229 cm), cut a 91" (231.5 cm) square from your sheet.

2. Fold fabric in half lengthwise and then crosswise into quarters, matching the raw edges.

3. Tie a string around a fabric marker. Measure a length of string (beginning at your marker) to half the diameter of your cut tablecloth. Using a T-pin, pin the end of the string to the folded corner of the tablecloth. Stretch the string taut and mark the outer edge of the circle. Cut along the marked line.

4. Turn up and fuse a narrow ½" (1.3 cm) single-fold hem at the bottom edge of the tablecloth.

5. Attach trim, if desired, along the hemmed edge of the tablecloth, using paper-backed fusible web (page 13) or fabric glue. Position the trim so the bottom is even with the bottom of the hem.

Make an elegant skirt for a round chair seat with a simple circle of sheer fabric. The skirt is made like a small round tablecloth. Use liquid fray preventer to prevent the fabric from fraying, or trim with pinking shears for an interesting edge finish. Place the fabric over the chair, allowing it to drape over the back supports. Tie 20" (51 cm) lengths of ribbon tightly around the fabric and back supports to hold the skirt in place.

> *Fusing*
> *Gluing*

SQUARE TABLE TOPPER

MATERIALS

Mediumweight linen

Four tassels

Fabric glue

Paper-backed fusible web or adhesive tape, 1/2" (1.3 cm) wide

1/2 yd. (0.5 m) contrasting fabric for monogram

1/2 yd. (0.5 m) paper-backed fusible web sheet

TOOLS

Tape measure

Marking pen

Scissors

Shears

Iron

Another clever way to use fusible web is to make a custom monogram to dress up linens like this square table topper. A table topper can also be decorated with fabric paints; stamp a single motif at each corner or a continuous row for a border design.

If a topper will be on a dining table, pick a fabric that launders well. If you use the topper on a side table, you probably don't have to worry about laundering, though you might want to put a round of glass on top.

To determine the size of your square table topper, measure the table diameter and add 16" to 20" (40.5 to 51 cm) for a pleasing drop length at the sides.

> *How to Make a Square Table Topper*

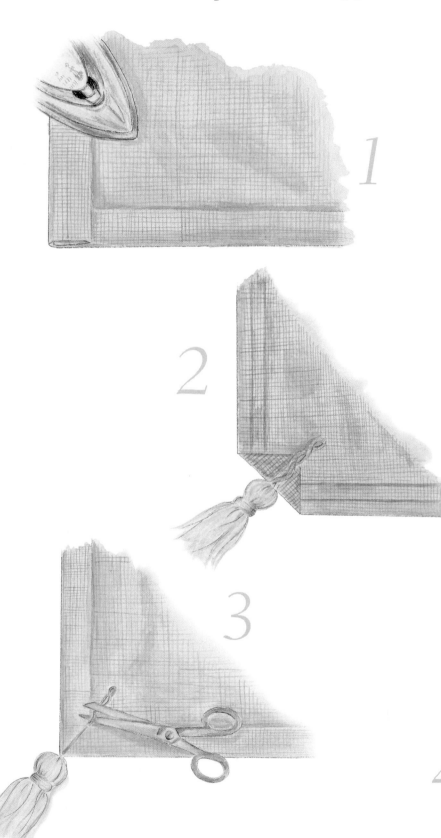

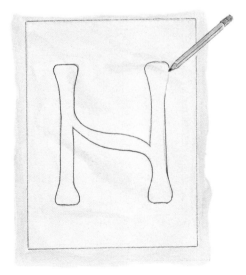

1. Cut the topper to the desired size square plus 2" (5 cm) for hems. Turn up and press (do not fuse) a ½" (1.3 cm) double-fold hem (page 12).

2. Open out the pressed edges. Turn in the corner diagonally and press. Glue tassel in place at the corner.

3. Refold the edges to make a mitered corner, using fusible web or adhesive tape to secure the hem in place. Trim excess cord on tassel.

4. Draw a pattern of your monogram on paper, 8" to 9" (20.5 to 23 cm) high. Cut it out. Flip the pattern over and trace its mirror image onto the paper side of the fusible web.

5. Fuse the traced web onto the wrong side of the monogram fabric.

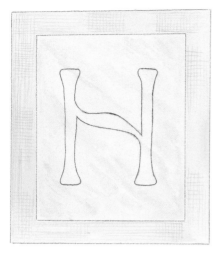

5

6. Cut the letter out around the marked line and remove the paper backing. Place the letter, web side down, on the right side of the tablecloth and fuse in place.

6

Table toppers are the perfect way to tie a room together. Make a simple topper with tassels as shown in steps 1 to 3, opposite. Use a fabric that appears elsewhere in the room or use a coordinating print. If the other room décor is fairly plain, make several toppers in seasonal colors and prints and change them throughout the year.

BED and BATH

> Padded Headboard

> Bed Cornice with
  Sheer Panels

> Gathered Bed Skirt

> Eyelet-Trimmed Sheets

> Shower Curtain

> Pom-pom Towels

> *Basic Carpentry*
> *Stapling*

PADDED HEADBOARD

MATERIALS

Decorator fabric; amount determined after planning headboard size and reading cutting directions

2 yd. (1.85 m) muslin or other lightweight fabric for backing

3 yd. (2.75 m) batting (or one package of queen-size quilt batting)

Plywood, 1/2" (1.3 cm) thick

Two 2 × 4 boards; length determined in step 2

Wood screws

TOOLS

Shears

Metal tape measure

Saw

Screwdriver

Staple gun and 3/8" (1 cm) staples

Iron

Pencil

Drill and drill bits

Bolts, washers, and nuts for attaching headboard to frame

A padded headboard can add a unique designer touch that is easy and inexpensive to make. It is simply a plywood base covered with batting and fabric. Headboards can be made for a bed of any size and can be designed with a straight or curved top. Your local home improvement store can cut the board to size for you.

Choose a fabric that will complement your bed linens. Your headboard may be wider than your fabric, as decorator fabric is usually 54" (137 cm) wide. Select a fabric with an all-over print (a small motif with no apparent direction), a solid, or a plaid. Fabric can then be railroaded to create a piece in the length needed (page 14). For best results, choose mediumweight to heavyweight decorator fabrics.

CUTTING

- For the headboard legs, cut two rectangles of decorator fabric 16" (40.5 cm) wide by the length of the legs plus 4" (10 cm).

- Cut decorator fabric 12" (30.5 cm) longer and wider than the headboard.

- Cut backing fabric the same length as the headboard but 5" (12.7 cm) narrower than the headboard.

- Cut two or three layers of batting 12" (30.5 cm) wider and 5" (12.7 cm) longer than the headboard.

BUILDING THE HEADBOARD

1. With your bed against the wall, measure from the top of the box spring to the desired headboard height. Next, measure the width of your bed. Cut your plywood to these dimensions.

2. Measure from the floor to the desired headboard height. Cut two 2 × 4s to this length for the headboard legs and back brace.

3. Place the 2 × 4s on a flat surface and lay the plywood on top so the 2 × 4s are flush with the top and side edges of the plywood. Using wood screws, screw the plywood to the 2 × 4s.

COVERING THE HEADBOARD

4. Place the headboard facedown on a flat surface. To cover the legs, fold under 1/2" (1.3 cm) on the upper edge of one of the fabric rectangles. Wrap the fabric around a leg, with the fold at the base of the headboard. Turn under the raw edge of the overlapping fabric and staple it in place. Start with a staple in the center of the leg, then add staples at the top and bottom. Fill in with additional staples.

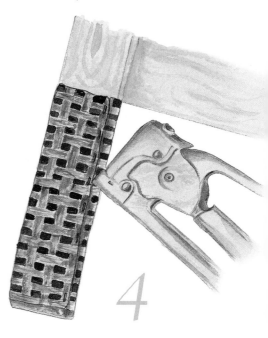

5. Fold the lower edge of the fabric over the leg bottom as if you were wrapping a package. Staple in place.

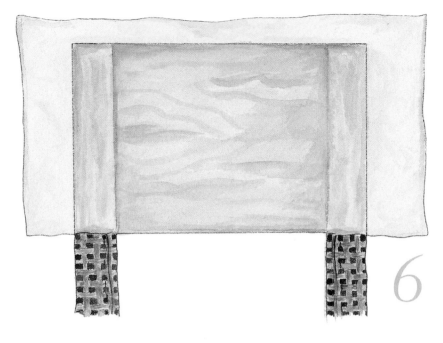

6. Place the batting on a flat surface. Lay the headboard facedown on the batting, aligning the lower edge of the headboard to the lower edge of the batting.

7. Wrap the batting around the headboard sides and staple in place. Continue wrapping the batting around the top of the headboard and stapling, trimming away bulk at corners as needed.

8. Lay the fabric, right side down, on a flat surface. Center the headboard facedown on the wrong side of the fabric. Beginning with the lower edge, wrap the fabric around the headboard and staple in place. Where the fabric meets the top of the covered legs, fold the edge of the fabric under the batting and staple in place. Secure the fabric along the headboard sides in the same way as the batting.

(continued)

9. Wrap the fabric around the top of the headboard and staple in place, beginning in the center and working out to each side. At the corners, miter the fabric (fold the edges diagonally) and staple in place. Trim away any excess fabric.

10. Turn under and press the edges of the backing fabric, so that it will cover the raw edges and staples on the headboard back. Trim away excess fabric to within 1" (2.5 cm) of the pressed edges. Place the backing fabric on the back of the headboard and staple in place close to the pressed edges.

11. Stand the headboard behind the bed frame and mark the placement for bolts that attach the headboard to the frame. Drill holes through the legs at marks, and insert bolts, washers, and nuts.

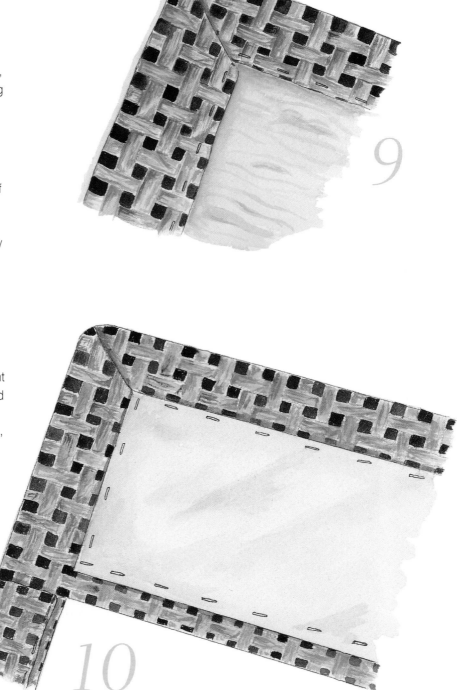

A DIFFERENT LOOK

A padded headboard is a fun way to decorate a child's room. In this little-girl version, the plywood base was cut in an arch. Designs that coordinated with the bedding were added with rubber stamps and fabric paint. To secure the fabric over a curved edge, begin stapling in the center of the curve. Work from the center to each side, smoothing the fabric over the edge and folding out the excess fabric into small, even tucks before stapling in place.

> *Basic Carpentry*
> *Fusing*
> *Gluing*

BED CORNICE WITH SHEER PANELS

MATERIALS

One sheet PVC or wood lattice

White paint, optional

1 × 6 board cut 2" to 4" (5 to 10 cm) wider than the bed

Sash rod

Heavy-duty adhesive-backed hook and loop tape

5 yd. (4.6 m) ribbon, 1" (2.5 cm) wide

Paper-backed adhesive tape, 1/2" (1.3 cm) wide

Two 5" × 5" (12.7 × 12.7 cm) angle brackets and screws

Sheer fabric, amount determined after making cornice

Paper-backed fusible web, 1/2" (1.3 cm) wide

Hook and loop tape

Silk ivy garland (optional)

TOOLS

Saw
Paintbrush, optional
Drill
Screwdriver
Shears
Tape measure
Pencil
Iron
Hot glue gun

A lattice bed cornice with sheer curtain panels brings the look of a summer garden inside. The cornice is made with purchased lattice. Wood lattice can be painted any color. If you want white, use PVC lattice, as we did here. You can trim the edges with ribbon or add wood molding.

Sheer fabrics are often much wider than traditional decorator fabrics, up to 120 inches (305 cm), so you can make the panels without sewing widths together. The sheer fabric we used here was printed with a pattern. Tulle is also a great alternative. The panels are attached to the cornice with hook and loop tape on the sides and a sash rod in back. They can be easily removed for cleaning.

BUILDING THE CORNICE

1. Cut two lattice pieces for the sides of the cornice 10" × 6" (25.5 × 15 cm). Cut one lattice piece for the front of the cornice 10" (25.5 cm) long and 2" to 4" (5 to 10 cm) wider than the bed. If you are using wood, paint it and allow it to dry.

2. Attach sash rod brackets 1" (2.5 cm) from the back corners of the 1 × 6. This side of the board will become the underside of the cornice.

3. Cut the heavy-duty hook and loop tape into 1" (2.5 cm) pieces. Remove backing from the loop side of the tape and adhere it to the back of the lattice at the top, at the point where the lattice strips cross. Place hook tape pieces along the narrow edge of the cornice board. (To be sure the tape pieces line up, mark the placement of the tape on the front edge of the board, using the lattice as a guide.) Attach the lattice to the board by joining the hook and loop strips.

4. Cut two strips of ribbon the height of the cornice. Fold the ribbon in half lengthwise and finger-press. Place two strips of paper-backed adhesive tape on the wrong side of the ribbon, finger-press in place, and remove backing. With the crease at the corner of the lattice, wrap the ribbon around the side edges of the cornice and finger-press in place.

5. Cut two lengths of ribbon equal to the side and front measurements of the cornice. Using paper-backed adhesive, attach the ribbon along the top and bottom edges of the cornice.

6. Attach the angle brackets to the underside of the cornice, aligning them to the back edge. Hold the cornice up to the wall and mark the placement for the screw holes. Remove the brackets from the cornice; attach them to the wall. Replace the cornice on the brackets and secure with screws.

CUTTING

- Cut two panels of fabric 8" (20.5 cm) wide by the required length plus 2" (5 cm) for hems. To determine panel length, measure from the top of the inside of the cornice to the floor.

- Cut one panel one-and-one-half to two times the width of the cornice by the required length plus 3" (7.5 cm) for the rod pocket and hem.

MAKING THE PANELS

7. Turn under and press a ¹/₂" (1.3 cm) double-fold hem on all edges of the side panels (page 12). Secure in place with ¹/₂" (1.3 cm) fusible web.

8. Using fusible web, attach the loop side of the hook and loop tape to the right side of the panels. (Loop tape can be applied in 2" [5 cm] pieces or as one long strip.)

9. Using a hot glue gun, attach the hook side of the tape to the top edge of the side lattice pieces inside the cornice. Hang the panels by joining the hook and loop tapes.

10. Turn under and press a ¹/₂" (1.3 cm) double-fold hem along the side and bottom edges of the back panel. Secure with ¹/₂" (1.3 cm) fusible web.

11. To form the rod pocket, turn under and press 1" (2.5 cm) at the top edge of the back panel. Turn under 1" (2.5 cm) again and press. Secure in place with fusible web along the inner fold.

12. Insert sash rod through pocket and hang panel from brackets along the back of the cornice. Glue pieces of ivy to the cornice, if desired.

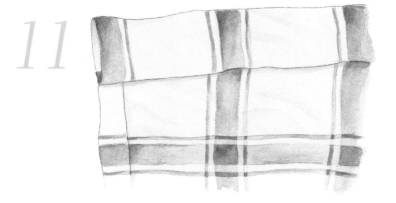

> *Fusing*
> *Gluing*

GATHERED BED SKIRT

MATERIALS

Mediumweight decorator fabric

Pencil pleat styling tape with looped back, 1¼" (3.2 cm) wide

Paper-backed fusible web, ½" (1.3 cm) wide

Hook and loop tape

TOOLS

Metal tape measure

Shears

Tape measure

Iron

Hot glue gun

A shirred bed skirt is the perfect finish to a bedding ensemble. This no-sew version is attached to the bed with hook and loop tape, making it easy to remove and replace. You may want to make several skirts and change them to match the linens you use in various seasons. The pleats are created with pencil pleat styling tape (page 11). This tape is available with a loop backing that sticks to the hook side of regular hook and loop tape.

The recommended fullness for a bed skirt is two-and-one-half times the measurement of each side of the bed. Because of this, the fabric will need to be pieced or seamed together to create a wide enough piece. To eliminate seaming, you can railroad the fabric (page 14), which allows you to cut two or three strips from one width of decorator fabric, depending on the length needed.

CUTTING

- Cut three skirt panels—one for each side and one for the foot of the bed. Each panel should be two-and-one-half times the length or width of the bed plus 4" (10 cm). Piece the fabric as in step 1, (at right), if necessary. To determine the drop length, measure from the top of the box spring to the floor and add 4½" (11.5 cm).

- Cut three lengths of pencil pleat tape, equal to each of the panels above.

1. To piece panels of fabric, turn under ½" (1.3 cm) on one side edge of the fabric and press it in place. Lay the folded edge over the raw edge of the adjoining panel and secure in place with fusible web.

2. Turn under and press ½" (1.3 cm) along the top edge of each panel.

3. Make a 2" (5 cm) double-fold hem on the bottom of the skirt panels and a 1" (2.5 cm) double-fold hem on the sides (page 12).

4

4. Turn under the ends of the pencil pleat tape 1/2" (1.3 cm). Attach fusible web tape along the upper and lower edges of the wrong side of the pleating tape. Then attach the pleating tape to the wrong side of each skirt panel about 1/4" (6 mm) below the top edge. Make sure the strings are not caught in the adhesive.

5. Knot the strings on one end of the pleating tape together. Pull up on the strings on the other end to pleat the fabric. Adjust the fabric to fit the side of the bed, and then tie the cords to hold the pleats in place.

6. Using a hot glue gun, attach the hook side of the hook and loop tape along the top edge of the box spring. Attach the skirt by joining the looped surface of the styling tape to the hook tape.

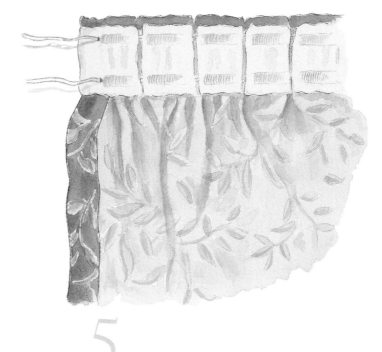

5

> *Fusing*
> *Making Bias Tape*

EYELET-TRIMMED SHEETS

MATERIALS

Flat sheet

Gathered eyelet trim, slightly wider than sheet hem; length equal to sheet width plus 1" (2.5 cm)

1½ yd. (1.4 m) printed fabric

Paper-backed fusible web, ¼" (6 mm) wide

TOOLS

Tape measure

Ruler

Shears

Bias tape maker in desired size

Iron

Gathered eyelet edging adds a charming touch to bed linens. You can cover the straight edge of the eyelet with custom bias tape—in this project, you'll learn how to make this trim from fabric. Or you could substitute purchased bias tape or washable ribbon. Preshrink the trim and fabric, and prewash the sheets to ensure that they will all behave the same when washed.

You can trim the edges of pillow cases the same way to make a matched set. For a coordinated look, add a decorator pillow made from the same fabric as the bias trim.

For the project as shown here, 3" (7.5 cm) eyelet edging was used to cover the existing 3" (7.5 cm) hem of the sheet. A 2" (5 cm) bias tape maker was used to make the wide floral trim.

CUTTING

- Cut a length of eyelet equal to the width of the sheet plus 1" (2.5 cm).

- To cut a bias strip of fabric, bring the cut edge of the fabric down to the selvage (finished edge of the fabric), forming a diagonal fold. Press the fold lightly. Open out the fabric; the fold is on the bias of the fabric. Cut the first strip using the fold as one edge. Each strip should be twice as wide as the desired finished width. You need enough trim to match the width of the sheet plus 1" (2.5 cm).

1. Place paper-backed fusible web along the stitching line on the top hem of the sheet. Fuse in place, and remove the paper backing.

2. Turn under and press ½" (1.3 cm) on each end of the eyelet. Lay the gathered edge of the eyelet over the tape and fuse in place.

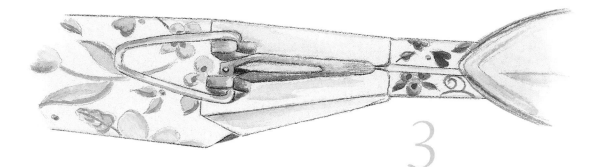

3. Run bias strips through the bias tape maker with the wrong side of the fabric facing up. Press raw edges in place.

4. Turn under and press ½" (1.3 cm) at each end of the bias strip. Fuse web tape to the folded edges of the bias strip; remove the paper backing.

5. Center the bias strip over the edge of the eyelet and fuse in place.

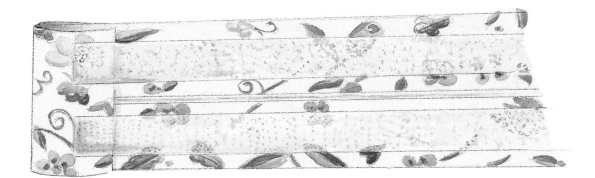

> *Fusing*
> *Attaching Grommets*

SHOWER CURTAIN

MATERIALS

Full-size flat sheet

Paper-backed fusible web, 1/2" (1.3 cm) wide

Twelve grommets

TOOLS

Tape measure

Shears

Iron

Fabric marker

Grommet setting tool

Ruler

A shower curtain can easily be made from a full-size flat sheet. If the sheet has a decorative hem, put it at the bottom of the shower curtain. Grommets are installed at the top for hanging the curtain.

Sheets aren't waterproof, of course, so you'll need a shower curtain liner. The directions that follow result in a decorative outer curtain that is slightly larger than a standard liner, which is 72" (183 cm) square. Be sure the curtain and liner have the same number of grommets so they can be hung together.

CUTTING

- Cut the sheet to the desired finished length plus 4" (10 cm).

1. Trim away the selvages (the narrow hems at the sides of the sheet), if desired, and make a 1" (2.5 cm) double-fold hem on each side, using paper-backed fusible web (page 12). Or use the full width of the sheet.

2. Make a 2" (5 cm) double-fold hem on the cut end of the sheet. This will become the top.

3. Mark the placement for the end grommets ¹/₂" (1.3 cm) down from the top edge and 1" (2.5 cm) in from each side. Measure the distance between the grommets. Divide this measurement by 11. Using a fabric marker, mark the placement for the remaining 10 grommets so they are spaced evenly along the upper edge.

4. Using the grommet setting tool, install the grommets at the marks (page 12).

SUPER-QUICK NO-SEW

Pom-pom Towels

1. Fold the towel in half crosswise. Using a fabric marker, randomly mark the placement of pom-poms between the fringe and the folded edge.

2. Glue the pom-poms in place at the markings, using a hot glue gun.

3. Place a strip of paper-backed adhesive tape along the woven band of the towel. Finger-press in place and remove the paper backing.

4. Turn under 1/2" (1.3 cm) at each end of the trim; lay the top edge of the trim over the adhesive tape and press with an iron to bond.

MATERIALS

Two hand towels

Two bath towels

50 pom-poms: 10 for each hand towel and 15 for each bath towel

Paper-backed adhesive tape or paper-backed fusible web

4 yd. (3.7 m) of trim

TOOLS

Fabric marker

Hot glue gun

Iron

> Gluing

FURNITURE and ACCESSORIES

> Framed Message Board

> Fringed Throw

> Fabric-Covered Lampshade

> Fabric-Bordered Rug

> Armoire with Fabric Insets

> Upholstered Ottoman

> Storage Table

> No-Sew Pillow with Wrap

> Photo Pillow

> Neckroll

> Tied Pillow Cover

> *Fusing*

FRAMED MESSAGE BOARD

MATERIALS

Picture frame

Mat board

Roll of cork

Carpet tape

Mediumweight decorator fabric

Paper-backed fusible web sheet (heavyweight)

TOOLS

Tape measure

Mat knife

Scissors

Iron

Turn a basic picture frame, a fabric remnant, and a bit of cork into a personalized message or bulletin board for your kitchen, craft room, child's room, or home office. When choosing a fabric, hold a scrap against the cork to be sure the cork does not show through the fabric or distort the color.

Cork can be purchased by the roll in craft stores and home improvement centers. Carpet tape has a strong adhesive on both sides and is available at hardware stores. Paper-backed fusible web is available in different weights and strengths. For the best bond, select heavy-duty or ultra-hold fusible web.

3

4

1. Remove the back of the picture frame and take out the cardboard support, matting (if there is one), and glass. Measure the length and width of the glass (be careful of sharp edges), then discard. Set aside the cardboard support, frame, and frame back.

2. Cut mat board to the measurement of the glass using a mat knife. Cut cork to 2" (5 cm) larger than the mat.

3. Remove the paper backing from one side of the carpet tape, and place a strip just inside each edge of the mat board and diagonally in the center of the mat to form an X.

4. Lay mat, tape side up, on a flat surface. Remove the remaining paper backing from the carpet tape and place the cork over the mat, pressing firmly with your hands. Trim the excess cork with a scissors.

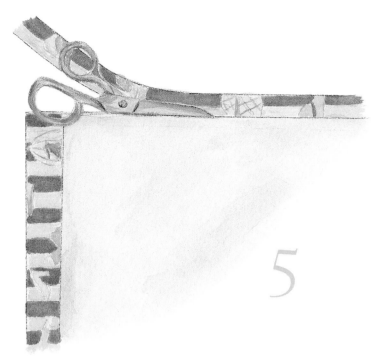

5. Cut fabric 1" (2.5 cm) larger than the mat board. Cut the fusible web to the measurement of the mat board. Center the fusible web on the wrong side of the fabric and fuse in place. Trim away excess fabric. Remove paper backing.

6. Place mat board, cork side up, on a flat surface. Place fabric, web side down, over cork, aligning the edges of the fabric to the edges of the cork. Fuse fabric in place with iron.

7. Insert the message board into the frame, placing cardboard support behind the message board. Attach the back of the frame.

> *Fusing*
> *Gluing*

FRINGED THROW

MATERIALS

1¾ yd. (1.6 m) of mediumweight wool or wool blend fabric, 60" (152.5 cm) wide

6¾ yd. (6.2 m) flat braid trim

Paper-backed fusible web, ½" (1.3 cm) wide

Liquid fray preventer

Four decorative bead tassels

Four buttons

TOOLS

Tape measure or ruler

Scissors

Iron

Hot glue gun

A throw is a stylish, cozy accessory. Choose a wool or wool-blend fabric or a fabric with similar texture that is loosely woven with thick yarns in both directions. For best results the fabric should be reversible. The fringe on this throw is created by fraying, or "unweaving," the fabric. The fusible web that secures the flat braid trim also prevents the fabric from raveling further. Tassels or charms can be used to decorate the corners.

It is important to cut the fabric on-grain, so that the fringed edges will be straight and even. The best way to ensure this is to pull out one or two yarns across the entire width of the fabric before cutting.

1. Pull out a yarn across the entire width of the fabric at one end. Cut through the center of the space left from the missing yarn to straighten the end of the fabric. Measure 56" (142 cm) from the straightened end, pull another yarn, and cut the opposite end. Cut away the selvages (tightly woven lengthwise edges) evenly, making a perfect 56" (142 cm) square.

2. Pull out a yarn 3" (7.5 cm) from one corner across the entire width of the fabric; pull two or three additional yarns along the same line to make it more visible. Repeat the process on each side of the fabric.

3. Remove or fray the yarns outside the pulled yarns on each side of the fabric. Lightly steam the frayed areas and trim the yarns to an even length, if necessary.

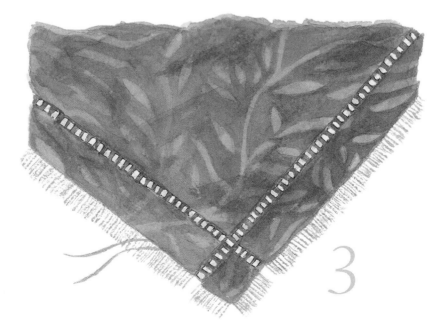

4. Apply trim just above the frayed edge, using fusible web (page 13). Cut trim diagonally at the corners, butting edges of trim together. To keep the edges of the trim from raveling, apply liquid fray preventer to the cut edges.

5. Attach a beaded tassel and a button at each corner of the trim with a hot glue gun.

> *Gluing*
> *Using Adhesive Material*

FABRIC-COVERED LAMPSHADE

MATERIALS

Masking tape

Wire lampshade frame

Paper-backed adhesive lampshade material

Mediumweight fabric

Gimp, 1/2" (1.3 cm) wide, enough to go around the top and bottom of the shade and along the sides of each panel

Quick-drying craft glue

Grosgrain ribbon, 5/8" (1.5 cm) wide, enough to go around the top and bottom edges of the shade

TOOLS

Pencil

Scissors

12 small bulldog clips

Adhesive-backed lampshade material makes it easy to create a custom fabric lampshade. Lampshade frames are available in a wide variety of shapes and sizes. Select the base of the lamp first, then select a shade that is the appropriate size for your base. Lampshade frames and the paper-backed adhesive material for covering them are available at craft stores, hobby stores, lamp stores, and online.

A fabric lampshade can complement a variety of decorating styles, depending on the fabrics and trims. A taffeta lampshade accented with beaded trim is very elegant. A checked cotton with brightly colored ball fringe creates a casual country look.

> How to Make a Fabric-Covered Lampshade

1. Wrap a piece of masking tape around the top edge of each section of the lampshade frame; number the sections 1, 2, 3, and 4.

2. Place lampshade material, paper side down, on a flat surface. Beginning with side 1, trace along the outside of the top, bottom, and left side edges of the frame. Trace inside the RIGHT side of the frame. Repeat with each section, numbering each traced area.

3. Cut panels just outside the marked lines. Check the fit of each panel, lining it up with its corresponding side. The panels should cover the entire wire section; trim the sides if the panels are too large.

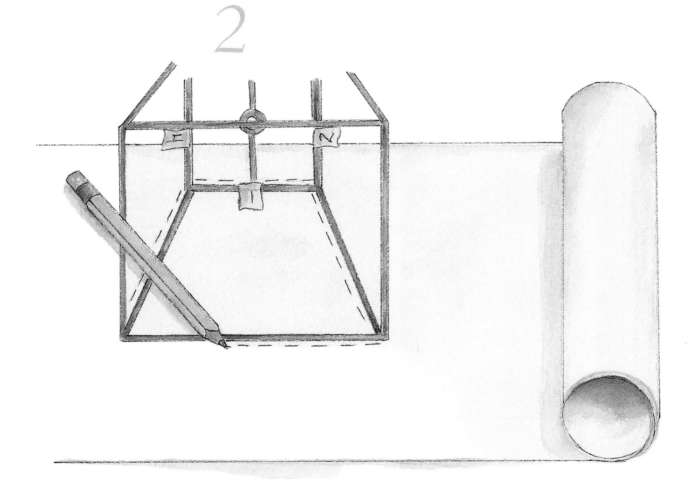

4

4. Lay fabric right side down on a flat surface. Place the panels on the fabric, and mark the top corners.

5. Remove the paper backing from panel 1 and place it, adhesive side down, on the wrong side of the fabric, matching the top edge of the panel to the markings. Smooth the fabric to remove any wrinkles or bubbles, and cut along the edges of the panel. Repeat with the remaining panels.

6. Remove the tape marker from the top of the first frame section. Run a thin line of craft glue along the wires of the frame section. Attach fabric panel 1 to the frame. Use bulldog clips at the top and bottom of the frame to hold the panel in place until the glue dries. Repeat with the remaining panels.

(continued)

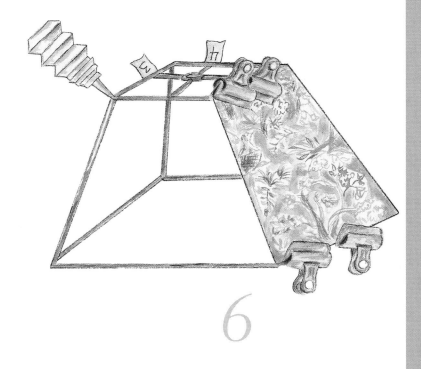

6

7. Remove the bulldog clips and trim away any excess material from the top and bottom of the shade.

8. Cut four lengths of gimp equal to the length of the sides of the panels. Center the gimp over each seam and glue in place.

9. Cut two lengths of grosgrain ribbon equal to the top and bottom measurements of the shade. Finger-press the ribbon in half lengthwise. Align the fold with the top edge of the shade and glue the ribbon in place, with half the ribbon on the shade and half extending beyond the shade. Clip the ribbon at the corners of the panels. Turn the ribbon to the inside of the frame and glue in place. Repeat with the bottom edge of the lampshade.

10. Cut two lengths of gimp equal to the top and bottom measurements of the shade. Glue gimp in place over the grosgrain ribbon, with the edge of the gimp even with the edges of the shade.

Top: Add a metallic touch to a purchased fabric lampshade with a decorative rubber stamp and good-quality fabric paint. Squeeze a small amount of paint onto a paper plate, then apply the paint to the stamp with a makeup sponge. This is called "loading the stamp" and gives you just the right amount of paint. Center the stamp on the side of the lampshade and press. Add a band of color to the top and bottom of the shade using paint and a thin paintbrush.

Bottom: For a quick round lampshade, buy an adhesive-backed lampshade made for this purpose. Simply peel away the paper covering and use it as a pattern to cut your fabric. Press the fabric onto the shade and finish with a bit of trim at the top and bottom edges.

> *Fusing*
> *Gluing*

FABRIC-BORDERED RUG

MATERIALS

Sisal rug

Mediumweight to heavyweight
decorator fabric

TOOLS

Tape measure

Scissors

Iron

Hot glue gun

Another clever way to decorate with fabric is to add a border to a sisal rug. If the rug will be in a high-traffic area like a living or family room, select a tapestry or upholstery-weight fabric. An accent rug in a bedroom can be bordered in a mediumweight fabric that matches or coordinates with other fabrics in the room.

Depending on the size of the rug, fabric bands may need to be pieced or seamed to make a long enough band. To eliminate or reduce seams on larger rugs, select a fabric that can be railroaded (page 14).

> *How to Make a Fabric-Bordered Rug*

CUTTING

- Cut two bands of fabric 7" (18 cm) wide and as long as the rug is wide plus 1" (2.5 cm).

- Cut two bands of fabric 7" (18 cm) wide and as long as the rug plus 1" (2.5 cm).

1. Fold fabric bands in half lengthwise, wrong sides together, and press. Open the fabric and press each long edge under ½" (1.3 cm).

2. Open one of the long bands of fabric and place it, right side down, on a flat surface. Center the rug over the fabric, aligning the long edge of the rug with the center fold of the band. Wrap the fabric to the front of the rug and glue with a hot glue gun. Turn under the raw edge at each end of the band as you glue.

3. Turn the rug over and glue the other edge of the band in place.

4. Repeat steps 2 and 3 for the other long side. Attach the bands to the short edges of the rug in the same manner, leaving the band free a few inches from each end. Lift the end of the band and fold the fabric under at an angle to miter the corner. Glue in place.

5. Turn rug over and miter the corner on the other side; glue in place.

> *Sponge Brushing*
> *Using Roller*

ARMOIRE WITH FABRIC INSETS

MATERIALS

Armoire with inset panels

White paint or primer

Acetate sheet

Mediumweight decorator fabric

Liquid starch

TOOLS

Paintbrush

Tape measure

Yardstick (meterstick)

Marker

Scissors

Chalk marker or fabric pencil

Sponge brush

Wallpaper roller

If you find (or own!) a cabinet or armoire with inset panels, you can use fabric to create a fresh new look.

The fabric is applied like wallpaper, using liquid starch. To ensure that the color of the cabinet will not show through the fabric, paint the inside of the panels with a few coats of flat white paint or primer. Let the paint dry thoroughly before attaching the fabric.

The best fabrics for this project are mediumweight decorator fabrics. Don't use chintz, since the starch will bead up on rather than saturate the fabric. An all-over print is the easiest to work with since the pattern does not have to match on each door. Cut plaids or checks along the same horizontal line so all the pieces match when they are applied to the doors.

> How to Make an Armoire with Fabric Insets

2

1. Measure the inside of each door panel to make sure measurements are the same. Cut a template of acetate to these dimensions. Check the fit of the acetate and adjust, if necessary.

2. Place fabric, right side up, on a flat surface. Place acetate template over the desired area of the fabric and trace along the outside edge of the template. Cut fabric along the marked line.

3. Remove the doors from the armoire and place them on a flat surface. Coat the inside of the panels with liquid starch. Apply the starch liberally with a sponge brush.

3

4. Place a fabric panel over the starch and smooth with your hand. The starch should seep through the fabric. Remove any air bubbles or wrinkles with a wallpaper roller.

5. Let the fabric dry thoroughly, about 25 to 30 minutes. If the fabric seems to be lifting, apply more starch and let it dry for another half hour or so.

6. Reattach the finished doors.

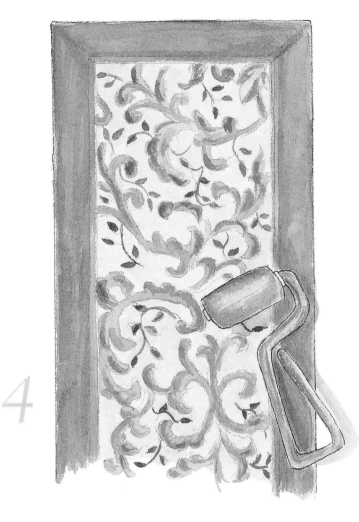

> *Fusing*
> *Stapling*

UPHOLSTERED OTTOMAN

MATERIALS

Plywood, 1/2" (1.3 cm) thick

Polyurethane foam,
6" (15 cm) thick

Spray upholstery adhesive

Medium- to heavyweight
decorator fabric

Upholstery batting,
1/2" (1.3 cm) thick

Muslin or other lightweight
fabric for backing

Leg brackets and screws

Legs

Bullion fringe (enough
to go around the outer
edge of the ottoman)

TOOLS

Tape measure

Shears

Pencil

Staple gun and 3/8"
(1 cm) staples

Iron

Screwdriver

Glue gun

An upholstered ottoman is a versatile piece for your living room or family room—footrest, extra seating, and, with the addition of a tray, even coffee table. It's easy and inexpensive to make the whole ottoman from scratch.

An ottoman is basically a plywood base and upholstery foam cut to size and covered with batting and fabric. If the piece will get a lot of use, make sure the fabric is durable. Choose a dense upholstery foam. Foam is sold up to 6" (15 cm) thick. If you need a thicker piece, you can layer two pieces with upholstery adhesive. The legs and leg brackets are sold in home improvement stores in many lengths and styles. They can be painted or stained.

The ottoman pictured is 25" × 35" (63.5 × 89 cm) and about 20" (51 cm) high.

> *How to Make an Upholstered Ottoman*

CUTTING

- Determine the size of your ottoman and have plywood and foam cut to specifications.

- Cut batting and fabric the length, width, and height of the ottoman plus 8" (20.5 cm).

- Cut backing to the measurement of the plywood.

1. Apply spray adhesive to one side of the foam. Affix the foam to the plywood.

2. Place upholstery batting on a flat surface. Center the ottoman, foam side down, on the batting. Mark the center point of each side of the ottoman. Wrap the batting and staple in place at each marking, as on page 84, step 4.

3. Staple every ³⁄₄" (2 cm) beginning at the center. At the corners, trim away excess batting and fold the corners under. Staple in place.

4. Place fabric, wrong side up, on a flat surface. Center the ottoman, batting side down, on the fabric. Staple the fabric in place at the marking on each side, as in step 2.

5. Continue stapling every ¹⁄₂" (1.3 cm) beginning at the center and ending 4" (10 cm) from the corners. At each corner, fold the end of the fabric, forming a diagonal fold into the corner. Staple fabric in place.

6. Turn the raw edge of the backing under and press with an iron. Staple the backing to the bottom of the ottoman.

7. Screw leg brackets in place on the underside of the ottoman, just inside the staples on the backing. Screw legs to the brackets.

8. Turn ottoman right side up. Beginning at the center back, glue the fringe in place along the lower edge of the ottoman.

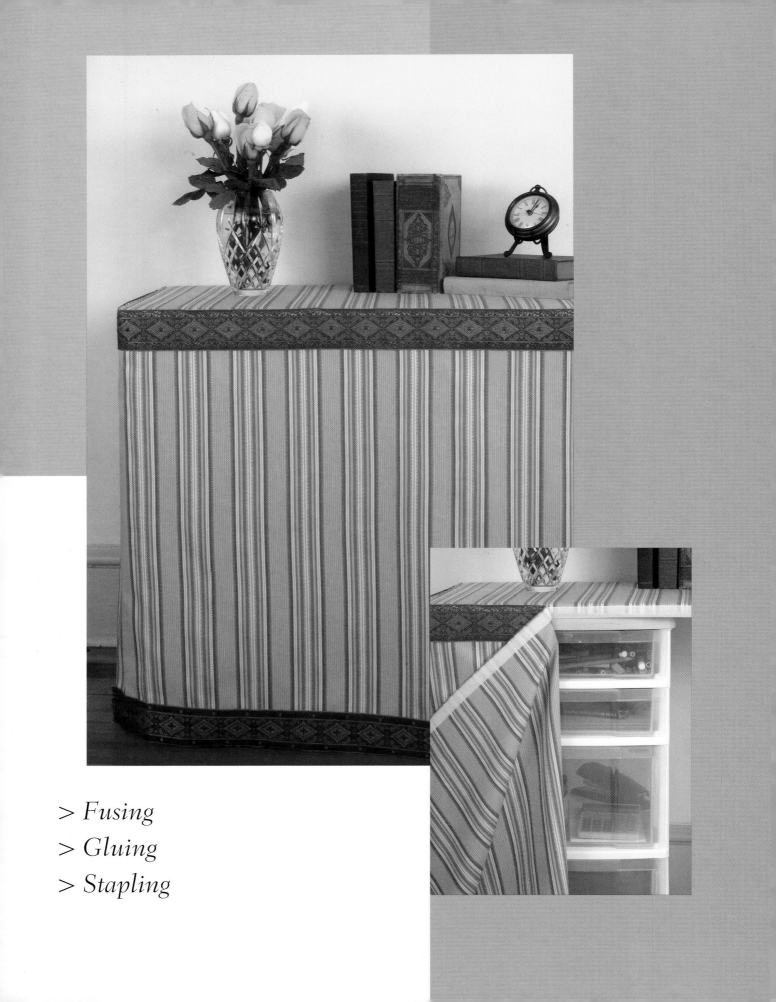

> *Fusing*
> *Gluing*
> *Stapling*

STORAGE TABLE

MATERIALS

Two storage units approximately
13" wide × 27" high × 15" deep
(33 × 68.5 × 38 cm)

Plywood, 1/2" (1.3 cm) thick, cut to the
depth of the bins plus 2" (5 cm) by
the desired length

3 1/2 yd. (3.2 m) mediumweight
decorator fabric

1 yd. (0.92 m) flannel or interlining

2 yd. (1.85 m) hook and loop tape,
1" (2.5 cm) wide

Liquid fabric adhesive

1/2 yd. (0.5 m) heavy-duty hook and
loop tape, 2" (5 cm) wide

Paper-backed fusible web,
3/4" (2 cm) wide

8 yd. (7.35 m) ribbon or decorative trim

TOOLS

Tape measure

Shears

Staple gun and 5/16"
(7.5 mm) staples

Iron

Plastic stackable drawer units are great for storing clutter, from toys to office supplies—but do you really want to look at them all the time? Keep them hidden but accessible with this clever table made of plywood and fabric.

A tailored table covered in a classic stripe with ribbon trim, as shown here, would be perfect for a family room or a den. For a child's room or a more feminine look, you can gather the skirt with styling tape (page 11). In a teen's room, the table can be topped with Plexiglas so treasures such as ticket stubs and photos can be displayed under it.

A layer of flannel or soft interlining is used as a buffer between the fabric and the wood, covering imperfections in the wood and making a smoother surface. The skirt is attached to the tabletop with hook and loop tape so it can be easily removed for access to the storage bins.

CUTTING

- Cut a piece of fabric and a piece of interlining twice as wide as the board plus 3" (7.5 cm) and as long as the board plus 3" (7.5 cm).

MAKING THE TABLE TOP

1. Lay fabric on a flat surface, right side down. Lay the interlining over the fabric.

2. Center the board on the interlining. Wrap the fabric around the long edges of the board and secure with staples, turning under the raw edge of the fabric. Fold the ends of the fabric in (as if wrapping a package) and secure with staples, turning under the raw edges of the fabric.

3. Cut two strips of heavy-duty hook and loop tape 2" (5 cm) shorter than the tabletop width. Remove the backing from the loop side and adhere the strips to the underside of the tabletop 6" (15 cm) from the ends. Staple for added strength.

4. Cut a length of 1" (2.5 cm) hook and loop tape to fit the front and sides of the tabletop. Attach the hook side of the tape to the tabletop edge, using liquid fabric adhesive. Allow to dry overnight.

5. Space the storage bins the desired distance apart. Check that the tabletop will fit squarely. Join the heavy-duty hook tapes to the loop tapes on the underside of the tabletop; remove the backing from the hook side. Place the tabletop onto the storage bins, adhering the hook tape to the bins.

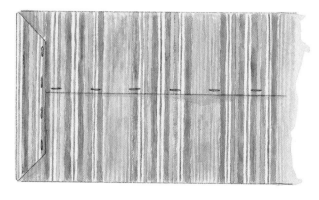

2

3

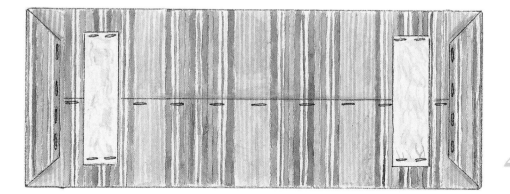

4

CUTTING

- Cut one skirt front as wide as the table front plus 1" (2.5 cm) and as long as the table height plus 4" (10 cm).

- Cut two skirt sides as wide as the table sides plus 3" (7.5 cm) and as long as the table height plus 4" (10 cm). Join the sides to the front to make one long panel, as in step 1 on page 100.

MAKING THE SKIRT

6. Make a 2" (5 cm) double-fold hem on all edges of the skirt, beginning with the top and bottom and ending with the side hems (page 12).

7. Attach the loop side of the 1" (2.5 cm) hook and loop tape to the wrong side of the upper edge of the skirt, using 3/4" (2 cm) paper-backed fusible web.

8. Attach ribbon or trim along the top and bottom edges of the right side of the skirt (page 13).

9. Attach the skirt to the table edge by joining the hook and loop tapes.

> *Fusing*
> *Gluing*

NO-SEW PILLOW WITH WRAP

MATERIALS

3/4 yd. (0.7 m) mediumweight decorator fabric

12" × 16" (30.5 × 40.5 cm) pillow form

Table runner

Paper-backed fusible web, 1/2" (1.3 cm) wide and 1" (2.5 cm) wide

Kit for making five covered buttons, 5/8" (1.5 cm) diameter

TOOLS

Yardstick (meterstick)

Tape measure

Scissors

Iron

Hot glue gun

Sometimes called "boudoir" pillows, these small, rectangular pillows are used as accents on beds. The blue floral inner pillow is made by fusing the edges of two fabric rectangles together, encasing a purchased pillow form—no sewing at all. The pillow is wrapped with a purchased white linen table runner that allows the pretty blue pattern to show through. Table runners vary in width and length. The outer edges can be folded under to allow the pillow ends to show more. Floral motifs were cut from leftover pillow fabric and used to cover the buttons that decorate the pillow front. Covered button kits, available in many sizes, include all the parts and instructions needed to make the buttons.

CUTTING

- Cut two 13" × 18" (33 × 46 cm) pieces of fabric for pillow.

- Measure circumference of the pillow and add 1½" (3.8 cm). Cut the table runner to this measurement along one short edge.

1. Turn under and press ½" (1.3 cm) to the wrong side of the fabric along all edges of the pillow pieces.

2. Place pillow pieces wrong sides together and fuse with paper-backed fusible web; leave an opening in the bottom edge for inserting the pillow form.

3. Insert the pillow form and fuse the opening closed.

4. Turn under and press ½" (1.3 cm) along the cut end of the table runner; fuse.

5. Turn under and press the desired amount along each long edge of the table runner, to allow the pillow ends to extend.

6. Wrap the table runner around the center of the pillow, overlapping the short edges; mark the overlap. Remove the wrap from the pillow and fuse in place with 1" (2.5 cm) tape, using a hot glue gun. Slide the pillow back inside the wrap.

6

7. Make covered buttons according to the manufacturer's directions. Glue in place along the end of the table runner, using a hot glue gun.

To make a tie-on pillow cover, follow steps 1 and 2, but leave one edge open. Turn under ½" (1.3 cm) and fuse. To make the fabric ties, cut two 2" × 9" (5 × 23 cm) strips of fabric for each set. Fold in the long edges ½" (1.3 cm), then fold the strips in half lengthwise and fuse the folded edges together. Fuse the ends to the underside of the opening.

> *Fusing*

PHOTO PILLOW

You can put a photograph or other image, such as a vintage postcard, on soft fabric, then use it to decorate a purchased pillow.

Your copy center can enlarge the photo and copy a reverse image onto transfer paper. Get specific pressing instructions from the copy shop (iron temperature setting, steam or dry iron, etc.) before you transfer the image onto fabric. It's a good idea to make duplicate copies of your image, so you can practice before making your final transfer. Put the image on 100 percent cotton fabric that has been prewashed to remove any finish that might repel ink.

If you have the right computer equipment, you can create the photo transfer at home, following the directions that come with the photo transfer paper.

CUTTING

- Cut muslin 1" (2.5 cm) larger than the image.

- Cut the fusible web sheet ½" (1.3 cm) larger than the image.

1. Enlarge image to the desired size. Print the image on transfer paper. Trim excess paper from image.

2. Place image facedown in the center of the muslin. Press as directed.

3. Fuse web to the back of the muslin, according to manufacturer's directions. Trim close to the edge of the image.

4. Remove the pillow insert. Center the image on the pillow front and cover with a press cloth. Fuse in place.

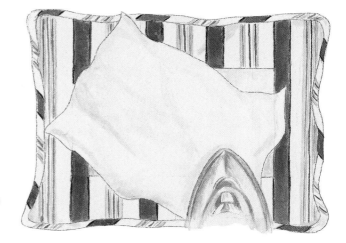

5.

5. Trim the edge of the image with gimp. Fuse in place (page 13). Replace the pillow insert.

A DIFFERENT LOOK

Decorator fabrics with distinct isolated images are perfect for accenting plain pillows. Simply cut the desired image from the fabric and fuse it to a piece of felt using paper-backed fusible web. Trim the edges of the felt with pinking shears, if desired, and attach it to the center of the pillow with fabric glue. Glue buttons at the corners.

> *Fusing*
> *Gluing*

NECKROLL

MATERIALS

1½ yd. (1.4 m)
decorator fabric

1½ yd. (1.4 m)
contrasting fabric for the
inside of the neckroll

Paper-backed fusible web,
½" (1.3 cm) wide

6 yd. (5.5 m) flat trim

Neckroll pillow form,
16" × 6" (40.5 × 15 cm)

1 yd. (0.92 m) cording

TOOLS

Tape measure

Shears

Iron

Glue gun

Neckrolls are small bolsters used as accents on beds or seats. This pillow cover is lined with a coordinating fabric that is visible at the tied ends where the fabric flares out like a candy wrapper. A decorative fringe fused to the flared ends finishes off the raw edges. You can buy neckroll pillow forms in several different lengths and diameters or make one by rolling a rectangle of upholstery batting to the desired size.

CUTTING

- Cut a 20" × 45" (51 × 115 cm) rectangle from each fabric. Note: The length of the fabric should run parallel to the tightly woven edges (also known as selvages).

1. Place fabric wrong sides together. Fuse in place along the two long edges.

2. Turn under ½" (1.3 cm) along each short end toward the contrasting or inner fabric. Fuse.

3. Fuse trim in place along the long edges of the outer fabric (page 13). Repeat with the contrasting side of the fabric.

4. Place fabric, outer fabric down, on a flat surface. Center the neckroll form along one short edge. Roll the fabric around the neckroll. Wrap cording around each end and tie. Place a bit of hot glue on each knot to secure.

SUPER-QUICK NO-SEW

Tied Pillow Cover

1. Measure and mark the placement of the grommets at each corner and at the midpoint of each side ½" (1.3 cm) from the edge.

2. Attach grommets at markings (page 12).

3. Cut lace into eight 9" (23 cm) lengths. Sandwich the pillow between the napkins, wrong side of the napkins against the pillow. Thread lace through the grommets and tie in place. Trim lace as needed.

MATERIALS

Ready-made pillow,
18" (46 cm) square

Two dinner-size napkins

Eight grommets

2 yd. (1.85 m) ribbon or lace,
½" (1.3 cm) wide

TOOLS

Ruler

Fabric marker

Grommet setting tool

Scissors

> Attaching Grommets

RESOURCES

The following companies provided products for the projects in this book:

All About Blanks
table runners, placemats
www.Allaboutblanks.com

Conso
decorator trims
www.conso.com

Fairfield Processing Corporation
pillow forms, batting

Jo-dee's
paper-backed adhesive tape
www.jodeesinc.com
(888) 888-1899

The Lampshade Shop
lampshade frames and supplies
www.lampshadeshop.com

Mundial
scissors
www.mundialusa.com

Rowenta
irons
www.rowenta.com

Rubber Stampede
stamps and paint
www.deltacrafts.com/
RubberStampede

Velcro USA
hook and loop fasteners and tape
www.velcro.com

Waverly
decorator fabric
www.waverly.com

INDEX

MORE FABRIC DÉCOR BOOKS

from Creative Publishing international

Look for these inspiring and informative books at your local
fabric and craft stores, home improvement centers, and bookstores.

Home Décor Sewing 101
A Beginner's Guide to Sewing for the Home

Sewing 101
A Beginner's Guide to Sewing

Bedrooms for Cool Kids
Clever Ideas and Practical Plans for Creating Imaginative Spaces

Windows with Ease
50 Fresh and Easy Ways to Dress Your Windows

Sewing for the Home
Over 50 Stylish Projects to Give Your Home a Fresh Look

More Sewing for the Home
Over 35 Sewing Projects to Beautify Your Home

Windows with Style
Do-it-Yourself Window Treatments

Do-It-Yourself Fabric Décor
Pillows, Window Treatments, and Slipcovers for Your Home

Upholstery Basics
from the Singer Sewing Reference Library

The New Step-by-Step Home Decorating Projects
from the Singer Sewing Reference Library